D1706234

A LEGENDARY TALE OF HOW A BORN-RESILIENT STREET ORPHAN SURVIVED THE URBAN CITY SYNDROME AND INCARCERATION IN THE POST-SLAVERY ERA OF AMERICA.

ANTHONY MCDUFFIE JR.

GRIT, GRIND AND GLORY

A legendary tale of how a born-resilient street orphan survived the urban city syndrome and incarceration in the post-slavery era of America.

Anthony McDuffie Jr.

Copyright 2022 Anthony McDuffie Jr, all rights reserved including the right to reproduce this book or portions thereof in any form whatsoever. No part of this book may be reproduced or transmitted in any form or by any means, electronic or mechanical, including photocopying, recording, or by any information storage and retrieval system without the written permission of the publisher, except for the inclusion of brief quotations in a review.

Cover and Interior Design by: JohnEdgar.Design

DISCLAIMER

The characters depicted in this book are fictitious. While some places and organizations may be real, the details are not true but figments of the author's imagination.

Any references to historical events, real people, or real places are created to the best of the author's memory. Some names may be used as synonyms to protect the anonymity of the individuals.

DEDICATION

I would like to dedicate this book to all the inner city youth, orphans, homeless men and women , prisoners, mental health patients, welfare recipients, those who struggle with addiction and all people who struggle through life trying to find hope and purpose for a better way of living.

I also would like to dedicate this book to my Mother and Father Charlette Frye and Anthony McDuffie Sr. Thank you for raising a Golden Child.

ANTHONY MCDUFFIE JR.

TABLE OF CONTENTS

ANTHONY MCDUFFIE JR.

INTRODUCTION

"THE BAD NEWS IS TIME FLIES. THE GOOD NEWS IS YOU'RE THE PILOT."
— MICHAEL ALTSHULER

Although I didn't know it at the time, I was at a crossroads when I was sixteen. I was home for the first time in a long time ; I was home for my first home pass from Los Angeles juvenile placement, where I had been sentenced to 9 months in juvenile camp after being refiled and kicked out for gang fights. I had to go to a juvenile boot camp for a strong armed robbery case.

I couldn't wait to go back to the hood and be around my brothers, my homies. I was sixteen years old at the time, wild and untamable. As with many teens, I felt like I knew it all and I felt unstoppable. I was involved in so many crimes in the neighborhood then. I was highly active in participating in gang banging.

Back then, I would wear my gang's colors almost all the time. Our color was red, so I put on my red pro club shirt, red shoe strings, and red belt buckle to match. I was representing the gang as much as I could.

I hopped on the 105 bus and landed right in the Baldwin Hills Village, aka "The Jungles." As soon as I landed, I was confronted by a respected homie.

"Blood, you know it's war right now with the 18 Streets, right?" He asked. It was the first I had heard of the war.

"You got on all this red, making yourself a target. You got your gun?" He continued with a tough tone.

"Nah, I don't have a gun," I said, dropping my head in shame. His disapproval seemed to hit me like a freight train.

He looked shocked, "You tripping, P Stone! Go get you one and take off all that red, or you are in violation!"

I realized right away that I was back in the trenches, in the South Los Angeles danger zone. I hadn't been in the hood in 6 months. That's a short while for some, but in the hood, it takes no time for the wars to intensify. I had one mission in mind: I needed to get a gun as soon as possible.

As I began to walk towards my big homie's house, I noticed a crash Gang Unit police force driving around the block. Now, I couldn't have any contact with the Gang Unit because that would have been an automatic violation of my probation conditions. No matter how deep into gang life I was, there was still room for common sense. For me, that common sense was to find a loophole.

I had to avoid them and travel through the street allies, aka "the cuts."I noticed a red Toyota caravan following me. Inside the caravan, a bald Mexican man was staring at me like I was prey. Based on what the homie just told me, I immediately figured out that this man registered me as an enemy . I had gone into a war unprepared and brighter than a neon sign; I was a walking target. I was watching the man's every move, and was sure that he was doing the same to me. My heart pounded as I tried to get as far as I could before the inevitable danger would strike. Every slap of my feet hitting the pavement sounded like a death march. I was hyper aware of myself, everyone and everything around me. It was this hyper focus that saved my life that day.

Suddenly, I heard a car door slam from behind me, so I quickly looked back. I noticed two hooded gunmen walking towards me with guns pointed at me. They both had aggressive stances, and their fingers were on the triggers. I didn't need all that to know they were serious, but once I knew for sure, there was only one thing an unarmed teenager could do.

Pop! Pop! Pop! Pop! Pop! Shots started ringing out, and I started running for my life. I ran down Hillcrest Street, zig-zagging and hoping not to get hit by a bullet. After being chased down a couple blocks, I got tired and hid behind a tree as the gunmen ran after me, trying to kill me. I stood behind the tree, too scared to even breathe properly, hoping they wouldn't see me. We were playing a dangerous game of hide and seek. By the grace of God, they ran right past me without noticing me. Once I was sure that they were truly gone, I slumped against the tree's trunk, my heart still beating wildly out of control as my brain finally processed the fact that I was temporarily safe. In that kind of volatile situation, most people who weren't involved in the gang war would stay off the streets and try to stay out of the war. That includes turning a blind eye to people in trouble, hiding wounded gang members, and hiding teenaged gang bangers. Fortunately, I met someone who did something unthinkable; she offered help. A woman noticed me hiding behind the tree. She spotted me from her apartment building windows and came to my aid.

"Oh my God! Oh my God! Are you okay?" said the frantic middle-aged Black woman. She trembled as she tried to help me up. Even then, I could tell that it had taken all her courage to leave the safety of her apartment to offer me aid.

"I'm okay, I'm okay. Thank you," I said with nervousness. I was trembling and scared at the moment because it was my first time getting shot at. About 16 shots were fired at me and I was spared. It was truly a miracle. I felt terrified as I got to my feet. My life had flashed before my eyes at that time, and I felt an unwillingness to simply let go. I felt like I hadn't lived long enough. I didn't know it then, but I faced an important decision.

The shooting shook me up a bit and made me feel vulnerable and helpless. Eventually, the feelings faded and the indecision about my life faded with them . Something more destructive replaced it; all I could think of was revenge. I believed that I had seen the worst thing that the gang war could throw at me. I thought that I was used to the sounds of close-range gunfire, so I was back to gang banging the next day like nothing happened. It was easy for me to fall back into the routine since I wasn't alone in this. This was the reality for many inner city youths throughout the county of Los Angeles. This was the life that we lived. The war had started, the streets had become savage and I went into predator mode. We all thought we were soldiers, and we could just roll through the traumatic experience. We even found ways to joke about it, feeling like it was a badge of honor to fight for our gang. Three weeks later, I would be involved in a gang-related shooting that would alter the course of my life.

Living and dying in LA wasn't just a cool catchphrase or a cliché, it was my reality. It was the reality that several thousand   Black and brown youths in the inner city faced every single day. Sadly, it felt like   an elaborate plan from the powers that be. I soon became part of the statistics of a failed race in the unforgiving society of America.

ANTHONY MCDUFFIE JR.

CHAPTER 1

NEGATIVE TURNING POINT

"THIS IS THE ULTIMATE WEAKNESS OF VIOLENCE: IT MULTIPLIES EVIL AND VIOLENCE IN THE UNIVERSE. IT DOESN'T SOLVE ANY PROBLEMS."
- MARTIN LUTHER KING, JR.

A Juvenile Hall fitness hearing is the process in which a minor is handed over to Adult Court to be tried as an adult for criminal charges. My charges happened to be four counts of attempted murder. At that moment, I didn't know what it meant to be tried as an adult. I vividly remember the expression and words said by the Asian American Juvenile Court Judge:

"I didn't want to do this, but I have to."

I was handed over to an adult court. The Los Angeles Superior Court had full authority to do what they wanted with my life. I pled guilty to 4 counts of attempted murder and was sentenced to 25 years in State Prison. A long enough punishment for my crimes, according to the leading DA of Los Angeles Superior Court. As a 17-year old, my young and frail mind thought that 25 years in State Prison was a life sentence. I had no idea how I was going to survive

1

the next day, let alone the next 25 years. I think my brain was still stuck on that and hadn't fully adapted to the gravity of the situation.

How did I get myself into this predicament? I wondered. I asked myself so many questions as I saw my life flashing before my eyes. I tried to evaluate my life and figure out where I had gone wrong, but at the time, I didn't have the maturity or the objectivity to actually do that. To me, it was like a death sentence.

I was born January 8, 1987 in a hospital in Lynwood California, growing up as a child in South Central Los Angeles. For the most part, I grew up in a stable household . My dad was a full-time work-ing man who supported the household by doing security work. My father would take my family to theme parks, outdoor adventures, and much more. He really did the best that he could. My father would provide for my other siblings, Paulette, Paul, Starkesha, and Mike. He bought them gifts despite their not being his biological children. My mother liked that I was very affectionate and passionate with my father. She would often refer to me as a "daddy's boy." A daddy's boy I was indeed. My father was very loving to me and my newest sibling at the time, Terell. Every birthday, me and my little sibling would be showered with gifts. I had the latest clothes and toys. I even got mon-etary gifts on most days. I remember falling asleep on my father's chest just about every night, which often felt warm and loving. My mother was a stay-at-home mom and provided safety for us as well. She was very loving and supportive.

We lived a decent life despite our living in abject poverty. Al-though we were poor, I never considered us poor because my moth-er did what she could to provide meals for us to eat every day and every night. If she got her county check between the first and 15th of every month, we ate well, but towards the end of the month we mostly ate scraps to fill our bellies. WIC was one of the main supporters. They provided County peanut butter, Cheerios, apple juice, grape juice, cheese, and if we're lucky, sandwich meat. My mother was not only a caring mother, she had her downfalls too. She battled drug addiction and struggled with it even before I was born. She also had a drama addiction. It seemed like she somehow always found herself in some type of drama, rather than fighting with the neighbors, family members, or boyfriends.

My father and I were already close, but we grew closer once his health started to decline. My father's eye sight deteriorated due to diabetes, and he lost sight in one eye. Something shifted. As my father stayed in and my mother continued going out to clubs and remaining involved in other social activities, something shifted. It began to feel like there were two sides to the house, and I was gravitating towards my father's. I was my father's caregiver, and he began to rely on me to assist him with basic tasks. I would often help him to the bathroom, feed him, and sometimes tuck him in at night. This formed a bond between us, and my mother's absence made me think that she was neglecting him. In my resentment, since I was closer to my father, I found myself pulling away from my mother . I had to step up to take care of my father. I was happy to help, but it took a part of my childhood away from me. I learned to be resentful too early in life.

Before my father's health declined, the cracks had begun to show in our family. It began with other attachments. My father had one with his ex-girlfriend and childhood sweetheart. My mother, of course, did not like the situation at all. For our family, this meant that a bitter rivalry ensued between the two women in the love triangle.

My father was in the middle of things, and he tried his best to bring the conflict to an end, but something soon happened that only made things worse. My father got his ex-girlfriend pregnant. For my mother, this was unwelcome news. It fueled the rise of verbal arguments in our family, and once the verbal arguments reached their peak, they evolved. Things got physical.

Domestic violence smeared the pretty image of our family's stability. I was six years old and constantly moved from city to city. I witnessed my father and mother have violent confrontations over relationship issues, finances, and trust issues. In this, I found myself biased towards my father. I didn't understand my mother, and I had no way to. I saw her as the source of our family's problems. No matter who I thought was to blame, the domestic violence worsened.

Sometimes, they were so violent that the police were called. There was a particular dispute that resulted in my mother calling the police on my father without his knowledge. I was the only one that was aware of what she did. I was my father's keeper, so I alerted my father immediately. Ultimately, this incident led to a split in the relationship my father had with my mother. My mother moved us to the valley, so I wouldn't see my father as often. I felt angered by the new set of circumstances and also by the environment that we found ourselves in. Before my father's health took a downward turn, he was the main source of providing for the household. Financial strain became an issue, and my mother's county check ended up being our main source of income. Financial woes weighed heavily on my mother. She started to stress over the smallest of things, which consequently led to her punishing me and my siblings. The stress she was facing snowballed, and I think we were an outlet. She got

4

abusive at times. I never saw it as a big deal; it was just "getting my ass whipped" to me.

Domestic violence formed another perpetual cycle in our household. Cycles can come in different forms, and in our home, domestic violence evolved until the children weren't excluded anymore. This time, it was with my mother and sister. Their different personalities and my sister's growing up meant that they would clash. I witnessed countless arguments between the two of them, which led to my sister's moving out of the household at a very young age. She brought in a new life without a clear vision for the future, so she went out in hopes of finding a better future for herself and her son. She wanted to make something better for herself and her son, which was admirable. Sometimes life forces your hand in ways that you could never imagine. Once my sister left the house, I looked up to my two older brothers.

Under the absent gaze of our mother, my two older brothers were introduced to gang culture. Even if my mother was around, she couldn't keep them from gang culture. It was all around us. Walking down the street, even going to a convenience store, our lives were soaked in gang culture. And like happy little sponges, my brother's soaked it all in. My brothers' fathers weren't present or involved in their parenting, and our mother was present but only partly. In the space between her bouts of parenting, my brothers would spend a lot of time on the streets with friends. Their friends introduced them to gang culture and crime. And since there was no authority figure to tell them otherwise, my brothers soon became part of a statistic, products of a bad environment. As their little tail and someone who thought everything they did was cool, I followed suit. I learnt gang behavior by watching and copying them. From how to dress, sag my pants, listen to rap music, how to speak, to how to be tough and have courage.

My attitude matched my mother's fire. We didn't get along much. I never cut her any slack and it seemed like the same went for her. I remember being at home one afternoon when I heard police sirens and helicopters. Hearing police sirens in our neighborhood wasn't a rarity, so we didn't realize that sirens were getting so close to our home. The police department burst through our door in military formation. My mother fearfully asked the police officers what was wrong. The police officers demanded for my mother to give up her first son and my older brother to their custody without knowing what the hell was going on.

My brother was just a teenager at the time. My older brother was placed in handcuffs and placed in the back of a patrol car. I didn't see him again for 22 years. He was inside a State Prison on suicide watch. They surmised that he was a threat to himself and others. I was told he had been arrested for murder. Allegedly, he was defending himself from a white man who drugged him and sexually assaulted him. I had no idea why he would go away for so long if that was the case, and it took a long time for the actual crime my brother committed to sink in. I was so confused. None of us understood what was happening. I couldn't stop myself from asking the question:

"How could my beloved brother kill someone?"

Spending the summer vacation at my paternal grandmothers house came with lots of benefits. My father stayed there with his mother, so I was able to spend some time with him. I was able to see my father and all of my cousins, uncles, aunties, and grandparents. It was really nice to bond with my extended family members. At my grandma's hosue, I learned many cultural beliefs and religious teachings . I also learnt how to be tough and brave around my cousins, because even appearing to be soft in their presence would be taken as a sign of weakness. It was a part of living there that I quickly came to accept. I knew I didn't want to be seen as weak. On average, there were at least 20 people there, and that was on a slow day. On a regular day, there were usually 40 or 50 people. It usually got really busy. It was fun, exciting, and fulfilling to be with so many family members.

Most of my cousins were from Compton and Watts, California, so being from these environments automatically made me insensitive to aggressive and violent behavior. My grandfather was overly aggressive when he used alcohol. He had an alcohol addiction, but his occasional violent episodes did not stop the family from gathering. Whenever he had his outbursts, we would regroup at another family member's home and laugh about the recent developments with my grandfather. If anyone felt uncomfortable with the situation, he/she would brush that feeling away. I know I did. I knew from experience that asking if our grandfather was okay would only earn me scoffs and a title as the weak cousin. Overall, I had an amazing time with my family on summer vacations. After summer vacations, I would return home to be with my siblings.

We didn't really know much about my maternal grandparents; my mother almost never talked about them. We had no idea if there was any bad blood between them. This was why we spent most of our time at my paternal grandparents' place. I still wish that my mother talked more about her side of the family .

My mother carried on living her overly social life. She and her friends would often go to nightclubs and other social gatherings. The responsibility of taking care of her kids while she was out having fun depended upon which friend or family member was available at the time. Little did she know that I was being sexually assaulted by one of her close friends' son. I was 5 years old at the time. I never told my mother about these incidents out of fear of not being believed or getting beaten. These incidents would shape my behavior for the next 20 years to come. Trust issues towards adults and male figures resulted from my terrible past with them.

I started getting into fights with kids inside the apartment building we lived in; I started stealing money from my mother's purse; and I became disruptive in general. I didn't feel like anything was wrong. Winning fights would give me a reputation, and other kids would know not to mess with me. It was a simplified version of something I had seen my brothers do on the streets.

My mother would take me and my little brother to my grandparents' house so that she could have the opportunity to be with her friends. Neglect was a feeling I had when she would leave us in a blink of an eye to go to a party with her friends. I felt more like I belonged to a family at my Grandparents house. It felt more like home there. I would return home to my mother only to be greeted by a new man inside our house. I always got so angry, but I knew that there was nothing I could do about it. I always felt betrayed by my mother whenever I saw a new stranger in the house. I would never approve of any man being with my mother besides my father. This made me more resistant to her, and she must have sensed that resistance. Perhaps my resentment was what widened the distance that grew between us.

My mother acted differently towards us whenever a man was around. I always realized the difference in her tone and manners towards us when a man was present. It almost felt as if she wanted to impress the man in front of us. That made me feel very undervalued and unwanted. I usually reacted by lashing out for attention.

Suddenly, my father became gravely ill and went into a diabetic coma. His conditions worsened by the day. It got so bad that my family was receiving calls from the doctor about taking him off the respiratory machine and ending his life.

The calm before the storm always seemed to happen when visiting my aunt. On this particular day, while visiting my auntie and playing with my cousins, I overheard a family discussion with the words, "We have to just pull the cord on him." Of course, I didn't fully understand these words at the time, and then a couple days later, my auntie told me that my father had passed away. I was just 8 years old at the time. I was devastated. I cried so much in the days leading up to the funeral. A couple weeks later, the funeral service for my father took place. It was such a sad day for me and the entire family. I was crying severely and I couldn't stop the tears from falling down my face. My father was gone.

To a child, death is a concept that eludes their understanding. The sheer permanence of death isn't something that any child should have to deal with. I couldn't grasp the idea that I would never see my father again, that I would never hear him talk, laugh, or hug him. I was heartbroken. This was the beginning of my negative turning point, the final straw that broke the camel's back.

ANTHONY MCDUFFIE JR.

CHAPTER 2

THE RUNAWAY

"THERE ARE MANY GOOD SEEDS IN YOU. THEREFORE YOU MUST
AVOID EVERY BAD SOIL IN THE WORLD.
- ISRAELMORE AYIVOR

My father's sudden passing hit me like a tsunami; it made me bitter and angry. I was stuck in a loop of constant anger. I used it to cope with the grief I felt deep within my soul. My life at home changed dramatically. My mother formed other relationships with other men soon after my father's death. Because my mother was so quick to move on and form other relationships, I felt that somehow she was responsible for my father's death, so I resented her and rebelled against her.

We would often clash over me disobeying her about one thing or the other. I continued to be a disruption and a problem at school. Whenever I was provoked, I would fight or become verbally abusive to other students. I would intentionally fail my class and not pay attention in school. By the fifth grade, towards the end of the school year, we moved back to Los Angeles, where I started junior high school.

Moving back to Los Angeles from the valley didn't just give me a shift in location, it also gave me a shift in my friend group. In the valley, most of my friends were Hispanic or White, and we had tame fun. We would play basketball and video games. However, in Los Angeles, my friends were all Black and with the location came a certain culture. These new friends were into sports, fashion, and girls.

Moving back to Los Angeles from the Valley exposed me to one of society's most persistent issues: racism. I remember approaching a cop car with two White officers inside that was stationed outside our house to ask them for baseball cards. The officer in the passenger seat smirked, reached into the glove department of the squad car, and handed me a picture of two lynched African slaves. They both laughed at the terrified expression on my face and drove off. From that day, I was immediately traumatized and distrusted Law Enforcement .

Junior high school in Los Angeles was interesting to me. I saw small cliques of students brutally attacking other students. I would see the students who got robbed of their lunch money getting teased by girls. It was a completely different environment, with its own set of rules. It was obvious to me immediately that fashion made you popular in school. I saw all of my peers get attention from girls by what they wore, not by how they looked. I noticed rap music was very popular and the main genre was 'shoot em up bang bang' Gangsta rap. It wasn't long before I started forming peer group associations. I began to make new friends with kids that I had a lot in common with. What I noticed at school was that all the troublemakers and gang members were really popular with all the girls. I wasn't noticed at all, but as soon as I started hanging around the troublemakers, the pretty girls in school started to notice me.

To help myself fit in, I became a class clown. The change didn't happen immediately, but I slowly began to form a pattern. The people around me influenced my behavior, and not for the better. An example of this is when a girl I had a crush on laughed at my Payless shoes. Fashion was a big thing in the school, so I felt humiliated. The pattern of behavior that surrounded me taught me that there was only one way to make right what I saw as a wrong; I went on a stealing spree. I stole some fashionable clothes and brand name shoes. My hard work paid off, as once my crush saw me wearing my newly stolen clothes, she complimented me. Her compliment was like a shot of dopamine. I was over the moon with glee. And I continued that pattern of behavior, contributing to the cycle that surrounded me when I first returned to the city.

The attention I received from girls my age made me feel good and accepted. I wanted to be accepted by girls and by my peers, so even at the age of 11, I would speak, dress, and act like all the troublemakers. As my peer association got even more negative, I started to become exposed to things I had never seen before, like drugs, gang fights, and guns. I started hearing languages that were foreign to me. The exposure excited me and made me curious about my friends from school becoming gang members.

In school, I met the people who brought me into gang life . It wasn't hard to join a gang, my friends at school all had gang ties or family members with gang ties. Sometimes I would run away from home and go to these friends' houses. On some level, I must have thought that their houses were like second homes to me. However, it was in their houses that I met gang members. Some of them would give us money to hold onto their drugs for a period of time, and others would introduce us to older women who took an interest in us. Sometimes that interest was sexual.

Despite this, I felt at home around them. It felt like they were my family; they would give me compliments and let me ride around in their cars. When I had run away from home and was going hungry, they would give me food and buy me clothes. Whatever red flags the gang culture raised that were flung to the back of my mind, I had found a sense of belonging with the gang members.

I saw firsthand how the gang culture seduced young Black and Brown boys at an alarming rate, and I was no exception. Slowly, yet surely, I was pulled into the risky lifestyle of a gang member. I strayed away with my friends into the Baldwin Hill Village, also known as the Jungles, the land of the Black P Stones.

The gang life came at a time when my life was very volatile. My home life was sitting on a powder keg, and whenever that keg exploded, I would simply run away. I had nowhere in particular that I was running to. I was searching for the illusory feeling of home, and I found it in the strangest of places. I wasn't the only teen out on the streets. Each year, an estimated 4.2 million youth and young adults experience homelessness, of which 700,000 are unaccompanied minors, meaning they are not part of a family or accompanied by a parent or guardian.

CHAPTER 3

GANGLAND STREET CODE

"SOMETIMES YOU HAVE TO PICK THE GUN UP TO PUT THE GUN DOWN."
- MALCOM X

Time passed and I went through my initiation. I became a member of the Black P Stones Nation; California district under the founder, T. Rodgers. The area where the Black P Stones settled would later be infamously known as "The Jungles," in Baldwin Hills, CA. It was once a middle-class haven for African-Americans, but it has become synonymous with gangs, drugs, and violence (hence earning it its lifelong name).

I was beaten by five other gang members inside an alley parking stall. I never understood why I had to be beaten to become a member of a brotherhood, but, like everyone else, I said nothing. I took the beating like a man. Immediately after the beating, I had to commit an act of violence on the enemy to prove my heart and commitment to the gang. I was taught the gang code and I was also taught how to represent the gang lifestyle. The process of socialization was rigorous and consistent. I learnt the fundamentals of how to be a gang member by mimicking everything gang related that I saw. I did everything to fit in, even harming people to prove myself as

ANTHONY MCDUFFIE JR.

an official member. I wore red hats and red belts with Black P Stone emblems, and I even changed the tone of my voice to make it sound more aggressive and intimidating when I hung around my peers. I felt accepted and I felt like each member of the gang was my family. I was seeking validation and attention from my gang members because I wasn't acknowledged at home. The older homies in the gang often asked me to do things for them. I looked up to them as father figures, so when they told me to do something, I did it without hesitation. I never questioned why we were at war with the Crips, Mexicans, or Police to begin with, nor did I question the objective of the wars. I just went along with the flow, escalating my act to fit in as time went on.

In most world wars, at least they had an objective for war, but in street wars there was no objective; It was just kill or be killed. Going to prison was probably buying you time until you ended up getting killed. Either way, your time will be lost. However, I didn't know that at the time. All I knew was the news that came from the people higher up in the gang hierarchy, and if they said we were at war with a certain gang, then we were at war. I later found out that most of the wars we were in were over women or drugs. I wasn't alone in the sea of ignorance. Most of my peers had no clue why we were at war;they just went along with it, and so did I, even when I knew the truth. We were simply foot soldiers, cannon fodder in a war that should never have begun in the first place. But we were happy. I was happy. Whenever I did something for the gang, it felt like I was protecting my family. The fact that I always got rewarded with praise when I did something violent helped reinforce that idea.

The praise was short-lived and superficial, but it made me feel special and more confident. It made me bold and brazen enough to continue to do more violent acts towards other rival gang members and people. In fact, I was encouraged to attack first most of the times. This led to me normalizing criminal activity and gang violence. I got locked up for robbery, and while in juvenile custody, I reinforced my vicious nature by attacking enemies on sight. This was the law of the land; juvenile hall was considered to be a gladiator school (it was kill or be killed).

I had grown to hate the enemy. My name began to gain a reputation inside of juvenile hall and outside on the streets. I had gained a notoriety that I became proud of. I saw it as a mark of honor, a stamp that proved all I had done for the gang. As an active member of the gang, I became a career criminal, going back-and-forth to juvenile hall from age 11 to 16 years old. Without sugar coating it, at this point, I had no regard for human life. I was evil, a criminal, a gang member, a liar, a manipulator, a drug dealer, and a violent, impulsive lowlife who was a threat to myself and others.

After a while, my mother kicked me out of the house for being rebellious and disruptive. I went to my friend's house, and their moms let me spend the night out of pity because I was out on the streets. I began making new friends quickly without even trying. Other Blood gangs were allies with the Village, so we shared common enemies.

Now, I wasn't new to the exposure of gangs given all my cousins were gang affiliated, but the difference was my new friends banged Bloods and all my family members banged Crip. In fact, most of my aunties and uncles banged or were affiliated with Grape Street Watts Crip, and my father was even alleged to be associated with Grape Street as well. According to the family, my father was the brother that my aunties called when there was a conflict. He was very protective of his family. He had leadership qualities that were noticed by the family. I was going against the grain of my family tree, yet I was fascinated by the new culture. Everything the Bloods did in the Village was bold and courageous.

They wore bright red, with Boston Brave hats or Saint Louis Cardinal hats. Everything about them was different from what I knew about the streets. I was embraced with open arms and given money and drugs to sell. One of the things I noticed right away was how popular the Bloods were within the community. They had all the girls, cars, money, and power. It seemed like everyone was representing the Village. I felt like I belonged, I felt at home, I felt embraced and I was finally acknowledged by the big homies. I felt seen. I began to represent the Village and attached myself to the Blood gang culture whole-heartedly. I hung out with the troublemakers by day and returned home for a few days, only to run away for weeks at a time. This became a repeated cycle. I would dress, talk, and behave just like my surroundings and shed my skin once I changed locations. I went through a brainwashing process because I began believing whole-heartedly in the 'Black P Stones Nation' creed and Blood ideology without question. I believed The Black Stones were superior to all gangs, and somehow, even the police. I noticed very quickly that violence was the fastest way to earn a reputation in the streets. The streets got very dangerous in an instant in my teenaged mindset. My enemies were clearly defined: Crips, Mexicans, and Police. They were the direct enemies, and we opposed them by any means necessary.

Being a gang member encouraged irrational thoughts, and these thoughts led to impulsive behaviors. You also had to worry about double crosses and triple crosses within the gang. Worrying about external threats while keeping an eye on internal strife was exhausting. Sometimes gang members had in-house fights , beefing with each other over money, girls, drugs, or jealousy. Often times, this led to a member being murdered by one of their own in the gang. These incidents became some of the coldest cases because sometimes foul play led to innocent people being killed because they weren't aware of the double cross.

I was given the name "Braze." I truly embodied the spirit of Braze and did brazen acts of violence to demonstrate and prove my commitment to the 'Black P Stones Nation' ideology. I was given a mentor, my big homie from the Village. His role was to guide, protect, and advise me. Not like a real mentor, he was more of an influence to make my path to crime smoother. Oftentimes, he told me to hustle to make a living, so I did. I sold crack, weed, powder, or even pills. I became addicted to hustling for two reasons:

One, for the thrill of negotiating something for something. I looked at it like a trade; I have a product for an exchange of your dollars. Secondly, I felt like I was lacking. I needed more if I was to survive as a runaway street orphan in the trenches. I didn't just need money; I needed power, and I needed a certain kind of reputation. I had seen people with money get robbed, and I believed that the only thing that could keep me and whatever money and property I had safe was undeniable strength.

In South Los Angeles, aka 'Ganglands', I witnessed so much violence that it altered my perception of humanity. My hatred for the opposition was present and waxing stronger every single day. The reality of being gunned down dawned on me, but it only fueled my emotions of hatred. I felt the hatred that came from seeking revenge. I felt the stress of the community when a member of the Village was murdered. And I channeled that stress into rage and hate. It felt like the only way to get rid of those feelings would be to inflict the same feelings on the enemy. I felt a lot of emotions that a child my age should have had nothing to do with.

A lot of evil takes place in the streets, and if you hang around demons long enough, you soon start behaving like them. I used to smoke weed, groove, and listen to rap music while riding around looking to avenge a fallen member of the Village. I would get fired up listening to lyrics that echoed how I felt in that moment. My mother warned me about listening to gangsta rap lyrics, but I never listened. She said that it was the devil's music. The lyrics of rapper 50 Cent in his song entitled "Many Men" were the words spinning around inside my head on autopilot:

"*I pop these punk niggas, like I pop my collar.*" These were lyrics I was living out through acts of violence on other Black and Brown people. I later learned that the word "music" is derived from the Greek word "mousike," which means "the art of the muses." The muses are Greek mythological entities that, according to ancient scribes, lived as nymphs that manifested as whispers in the ears of poets and whoever else invoked them. They would sway and inspire men to do as they desired, too. The muses that whispered in my ears were evil, and their songs made me a murderous delinquent. In fact, everybody around me danced to the same murder drum.

I always kept a gun and prepared to the best of my ability for gun battles. I was taught to take the charge, so becoming a shooter for the members was in the works for me. Everyone in my circle had guns. I remember having a bucket full of bullets inside an abandoned apartment building and loading up semi-automatics. It was like a war merchant made a deal with the devil and chose the lower

Baldwin Hill Village as the landing dump for some of the deadliest assault rifles known to the streets of South Los Angeles. This would definetly ignite gang wars with homicides, claiming the lives of several young Black and Brown boys for the next generation to come. I was no exception to the statistics of violent crimes being committed on Black people by Black people.

In 2004, my codefendant picked me up to spend time with him after going through the loss of his grandfather. When I started talking to him about his grandfather's death, it made me feel sad because I related it to the death of my own father. The memory made me feel the pain, so much pain that I wanted to hurt someone because I was hurting inside. He drove me through a rival neighborhood in the Village, where a gang was allegedly responsible for the killing of our beloved friend and member of the Village, Baby Ace. I wanted to avenge his murder, that was my only thought process as I held a Glock 40 automatic handgun. I noticed four people who appeared to be gang members and opened fire, striking all four with the intent to kill. I deliberately looked to inflict harm on a person who looked just like myself, a young person with their whole life ahead of them. I intentionally went out to cause terror and commit mass injury to another Black community. I was so disconnected from humanity that I couldn't see my way back. I was apathetic and unapologetic. I didn't care about the families of the people that I hurt; I just wanted to get revenge regardless of the consequences. The streets made me cold-hearted and hateful. The streets made me a monster.

CHAPTER 4

THE LOS ANGELES COUNTY JAIL

"WE MUST ACCEPT FINITE DISAPPOINTMENT, BUT NEVER LOSE INFINITE HOPE."
– MARTIN LUTHER KING, JR.

Blacks and Hispanics make up a larger share of the U.S. prison population. In 2017, Black people represented 12% of the adult population but made up 33% of the sentenced population. However, white people made up 65% of the adult population but accounted for 30% of the sentenced population. What I'm trying to say is that the odds were against me the moment I had to appear before a judge.

I was tried as an adult at the age of seventeen., I had done bad things, but I was still young. I was moved to an adult court from juvenile hall to the county jail in Los Angeles. This experience, to me, was like surviving on an abandoned island. I was scared, but there was nothing I could do. I was stuck in this situation at the young age of seventeen. There wasn't anyone or anything to guide me through this. I was lonely. I was left feeling vulnerable and abandoned, but there was nothing I could do. In a way, I felt like I deserved my time there. My mind went back to all the things I could have done differently, the paths I could have crossed, the lives I could have impacted positively. When I caught myself in this train of thought, I stopped because it wasn't doing any favors for my mental health. I realized early in my stay there that there was no use in crying over spilt milk or dwelling on the past.

The Los Angeles county jail was a truly terrifying place. There were different types of people there, from minor to major crimes. They were all lumped together like sardines crammed into a can. There was a wide spectrum of every human rights violator known to man. It was a cesspool of criminality, a breeding ground for racist ideologists, and a safe haven for some of California's most notorious street gangs. I was thrown into the lion's den, and the only thing I had at that time was my heart and a street gang mentality.

I was placed in a holding cell with at least fifty men. These men were mostly homeless, so the odor of 50 men compacted inside a holding tank made breathing extremely harsh. The odor smelled like a rotten corpse. I felt like I was losing oxygen.

We had routine mandatory searches almost every day. It was a way to make sure that we weren't sneaking any prohibited substances. The normal procedure here was to debase you by exposing your rectum every day for those mandatory searches. It got dehumanizing fast, but this was the routine and I got used to it. I felt embarrassed to get naked in front of these men. I didn't want these men to see my private parts. My cell was very uncomfortable. Every object around me felt hard and unsafe. The walls were tall in structure and a dirty white color from years of neglect by the cleaning services that were in charge.

The floors were concrete, with scum and scuff marks splattered everywhere. The jail bars were gray and made of concrete. Images of John Wayne the Cowboy were on the hallway walls and I often wondered why. I later found out that he was an American actor praised for his roles of murdering Native Americans. Throughout most of his life, Wayne was a prominent and vocal conservative Republican in Hollywood, supporting anti-communist positions. But why was he on the hallway walls of a male county jail? It definitely had a racial undertone, and I didn't like it. But there was no time to focus on what I liked and hated, especially since I couldn't change anything.

The sheriffs were tyrants. They patrolled the county jail like lunatics, yelling in the faces of men, cursing them, beating them, provoking them, and oppressing them. Every day, I saw the county jail sheriffs break the spirits of different men. This was a violence that reached across race and only looked at two things: those behind bars, and those wearing the uniform. It was violence that we had no way of resisting, as that would only make our cases worse. One day, my cellmate, a Hispanic Sureno gang member from the Harbor Area, talked to a Hispanic deputy in charge of our cell block. The officer returned a couple hours later to pull my cellmate out of the cell and escort him handcuffed towards the dirty shower area. I watched from my cell as the deputy handcuffed my cellmate's hands to the shower bar and proceeded to beat him down with a long metal flashlight.

The sounds of his cry of agony made me cringe. Something shifted in my spirit that day. I was shocked. I didn't think a deputy would just deliberately and unapologetically beat a man in front of everybody. They had no fear because they knew that there was nothing we could do about it. There were no consequences for their actions, and there was no justice for the injuries they would inflict on us. I was traumatized and afraid at the same time. I wondered if that would one day be my fate. The food was terrible. Breakfast consisted of half-cooked boiled eggs, a kid's bowl of cereal, two stale pieces of bread, and milk. Lunch was a sack lunch with baloney, two pieces of stale bread, and a sugary flavored drink. Dinner consisted of slop. It was quite literally slop; you couldn't make out what was inside of the food or what type of meat it was. The water we drank from out of the faucet most of the time had turned gray and sometimes was even brown. They gave us instant coffee, but it tasted like dirt with hot water. It was so disgusting. Other brands of coffee were purchased through the commissary, which means we had to buy it from the county jail store. The brand that was mostly available was called 'Keefe.'

My first experience with coffee was in a six-man cell with a couple of homies from West Side Piru in Compton. We usually drank coffee to stay up, tell war stories, rap our favorite songs, and sometimes prepare for war. My young juvenile mind now had to adjust to my new surroundings and the new institution. It was not a game, like I thought juvenile hall was. I was surrounded by men who were older than I was, and no matter how tough I thought I was, they were tougher. They had seen more; they were battle-hardened. The men all around me had the mentality to harm the next man given the word. In the county jail, you were forced into a 'kill or be killed' mode. I refused to be prey, so I prepared myself for a battle of any kind. Even though I did not know how to prepare myself efficiently and properly, I just did what I saw my older homies do to survive, and that was stay on the offensive by exercising, sharpening manufactured prison knives, reading war books, and staying alert. I could never let my guard down, not even when I was asleep. It was a good way to get seriously injured or killed.

I remember the first time I heard and felt the presence of the Southern United Raza, also known as the "Sureneos." They consisted of all Southern Mexican street gangs combined under the rule of the Mexican Mafia. At the time, I didn't understand how organized and powerful they were. I later found out through a series of riots that transpired throughout the whole county jail. Growing up in South Los Angeles, I knew that racism existed, but entering the county jail was another form of racism that I had never experienced before. It was an "in your face" type of racism, like someone was constantly shoving it down your throat. Mexicans in the Los Angeles county jail were considered enemies of the Blacks.

This was when I witnessed and experienced segregation like no other. Mexicans and Blacks couldn't eat from the same plate as one another, nor could they play with one another. State phones were divided, tables were divided, and recreational spaces were divided. Not only were we bound to the dictation of the county jail authorities, but also by the politics of our own groups. We were people facing an external threat but, we couldn't stop ourselves from in-fighting.

County jail sheriffs were known to incite riots between Mexicans and Blacks. To them, it was very amusing to observe the violence that transpired between us. We weren't people to them, we were entertainment. Something as simple as a breakfast burrito could be the bait that instigated a full-scale riot. County jail sheriffs are only a microcosm of a macrocosm of a system of racial stratification. The stratification is related to ways in which people in communities, societies, or nations earn a living through pyramid schemes. Those on the bottom look up to the top for survival. Minorities depend on a system which therefore puts them in an ascribed status or born into reality to depend on the government for their livelihood.

This class system strategy creates a racial caste system which produces slavery, segregation, and deconstruction of people to subject them to disease, crime, self-victimization, homicide, infant mortality, ghettos, jails, prisons, and mental asylums. The Department of Rehabilitations (CDC) and all its agents are systematically in place to further disenfranchise the Black and Brown community. Deprivation of any kind is a hindrance to the overall wellbeing of humans. In the county jail, they restricted me from even being social with ordinary people. As a result of this, I became socially awkward . Deprivation can easily turn into desperation for an incarcerated person. Because of being deprived for so many years, I experienced feeling desperate to the point of extorting people for basic necessities like toilet paper, toothpaste, and food items. Deprivation also led me into depression. Oftentimes, I felt depressed about my circumstances and did not have the energy to even want to communicate with anyone. =During those times, I would drink coffee and read books. Depression also altered my mood and appetite. I wouldn't eat anything nutritional, but instead snacked on all sorts of unhealthy snacks to soothe my spirit and fall asleep. I would wake up to instant coffee packs. The coffee was so horrible that I had to add chocolate powder to my cup to give it a pleasant taste. Coffee was used inside the county jail as a commodity of trade. Inmates would exchange it for drugs, food items, or favors. At the time, I consumed coffee for social interactions and staying awake in case I had to participate in a full-scale riot.

'48 Laws of Power' and 'The Art of Seduction' by Robert Greene were popular books that were read inside the county jail. I also began to read these books to further my reading comprehension. I noticed right away how the '48 Laws of Power' was a book most inmates used to teach manipulation. I began to learn the art of finesse by watching my older homies play county jail politics with other races to control the flow of drugs or to take the offense in war. There was war, and I didn't have a choice of which side I was on. Being a Blood in the county jail automatically locked me into a political affiliation. I was now under the dictates of a tribal order.

"Nothing is bigger than the B" were popular words uttered by the members of the gang. It was a brainwashing technique used for conformity. Disciplinary actions by any of the members were done in public for display, to showcase power, control, and incite fear into the hearts of the enemies and rebels within the ranks. I witnessed violence taking place regularly. I was placed in holding tanks to await court, surrounded by Southern Mexicans. I would get jumped on and beat by several Hispanic men in one tank, go inside the courtroom to see the judge for 10 minutes only for him to postpone my hearing, and plot to avenge myself in another tank within a 30 minute time frame. I got jumped on and brutally beaten at least three times inside the LA County jail by Southern Mexican gang members. It added to the hate I had at the time for Southern Mexican gangs and added to the compounded trauma I was already experiencing from my adverse childhood experience. In this fight or flight mindset, I became very untrusting and suspicious of people outside the gang. My warped mentality made me think that if you weren't in a gang, then you weren't worth trusting . This principle proved to be contradictory when I got snitched on by a homie. In the business world, I learnt that you must be willing to negotiate business even with an enemy if the price is right. In the business world, you would even be willing to cut blood-related ties because of bad business.

The Los Angeles County jail was teaching me hard lessons and transferable skills. I would later use these skills to finesse my way through the system. I knew this journey was about to come with trials and tribulations. At 3 a.m. , county jail sheriffs raided our cell like we were part of a sting operation. They pointed Taser guns at our faces and demanded that we strip naked for a search. After they began a thorough search of our bodies and cells, they found 13 prison manufactured knives and sent me and the rest of the homies to a segregated housing unit, aka the hole. Because the hole was overcrowded and packed to the brim, I was forced to have multiple cellmates that I had to be confined to 24 hours a day. Men placed in these kinds of stressful situations often kill their cellmates or kill themselves. There have been several cases of this happening. I also realized they split all of the homies up, so now I was surrounded by Crips, Southern Mexicans, and a few Whites. Being away from the support and protection of the homies made me realize real quick that the tables can turn in a snap of a finger and you can be surrounded by enemies faster than you can blink. I had to stand tall and represent the gang by showing no sign of fear, but I was very scared; after all, I was still a child. I was constantly alert and constantly scared, living day by day and only thinking about how to get by. I was stuck in a sort of fight or flight existence while at the same time dealing with horrible living conditions.

The segregated housing unit never got cleaned, unlike my previous accommodations. The unit was so filthy that we had a rat infestation. The inmates would nickname the rats "Freeway Freddys" because they ran across the floor so often it was like they were on a freeway. The rats would bite inmates and raid their store bags, eating their food. Men were catching staph infections left and right from the unsanitized living quarters, but the Warden and Sheriffs did not care. To them, we were not worth any effort. The Los Angeles

County jail felt and operated like the middle passage to modern-day slavery. It was my own personal hell.

ANTHONY MCDUFFIE JR.

CHAPTER 5

FIRST DAY OF PRISON

"SUCCESS IS NOT FINAL, FAILURE IS NOT FATAL:
IT IS THE COURAGE TO CONTINUE THAT COUNTS."
— WINSTON CHURCHILL

"Anthony McDuffie #83726, roll up your property, you're catching the chain".

I heard my name over the intercom of the Los Angeles County jail segregated housing unit. I was to be transported to a state prison. Strangely enough, I was excited about going to prison. The county jail functioned like a middle passage for slavery. It was designed to break the spirits of men to the point they were willing to cop out and plead guilty, sometimes to offenses that they didn't even commit, only to get to prison to receive somewhat better treatment. I was shackled from my ankles all the way to my wrist by a group of men I had never seen before. I was stripped out, meaning I had to get completely naked and get searched for weapons or drugs. After these searches, the department of corrections officers began to give us an unpleasant speech about the rules of the bus ride.

"We don't give you a warning shot, we just shoot you dead and that will be that," said a muscular, tattooed Hispanic correctional officer with a cold-hearted demeanor and an even colder tone. He was accompanied by another White correctional officer, tattooed and intense just like he was. They looked at us with harsh gazes, and I knew instinctively that there was no such thing as a second chance in their books. It felt like even breathing wrong could get me on the wrong end of a gun.

Despite how uncomfortable I felt and the feelings of rebellion that I saw clearly on the faces of other prisoners, we fell in line. We boarded the prison bus, which was so uncomfortable. It was made of metal and it made my ass ache. It was cold too and did nothing to dispel the freezing weather. Shackled, stiff, cold, and uncomfortable, the ride felt like I was on a slave ship. I felt a high level of anxiety while riding on that bus for hours. I remember thinking about the lessons of conduct I received from other inmates about prison. Their major lesson was the 3 L's: 'Look, Listen, and Learn.' These three simple but important tools would become very useful to me in the end. Another lesson was to never let a man play with you sexually. In the confined space of prison, locked away from other people, the rules were different. They had taken us away from society, but we still had needs building up. For many, the outlet for their needs was unhealthy and manipulative. I saw how predatory men played on the vulnerabilities of timid men and ended up sexually assaulting them. I felt that as a 19-year-old, I was even more vulnerable. I was obviously younger than most people there.

When I arrived at Lancaster State Prison, I was rushed off the bus by about five intimidating white correctional officers yelling at us as if we were new cadets entering into military boot camp. I later learnt that it was part of a scare tactic used by CDCR to incite fear in the hearts of inmates so that they had to comply with the authorities, similar to the tactics used to break the spirits of slaves during the time of slavery. =I submitted myself to yet another mandatory search. I was then given a ziplock baggie equipped with one razor, one tiny bar of soap, a plastic black comb, a one-inch toothbrush, and one small tube of toothpaste, along with two sheets and a blanket made of wool that irritated my skin. I was placed in a two-man cell with an older brother whose name I can't recall at the moment, but he didn't belong to any gang affiliation. Because I was inside the gang files and registered as an active gang member, the CDCR administration set up an arbitrary rule to only pair me up with other Bloods or non-gang affiliates. This rule was made in part to control tension and maintain order within the prison. A Blood and Crip made to be cellmates doesn't always turn out safe. That can in fact be very dangerous. We introduced each other and shared pictures of our families . Picture sharing amongst inmates is a common thing done amongst cellmates in prison to open up and form some type of relationship. Respect was given to every man, unless you snitched on someone, or you went into protective custody for whatever reason.

We played cards together, shared food with each other, and looked out for each other. I remember him telling me that I wasn't going to serve all of my time. He was a religious man and talked a lot about God . I remember him reading biblical scriptures to me, reminding me of the good news. I felt a weird sense of hope whenever I heard his words. He also wrote me a poem that I faintly remember. Before long, he left on his journey, but a part of him stayed in the cell with me.

ANTHONY MCDUFFIE JR.

CHAPTER 6

THE CREATION OF THE COFFEE BALLS

"NO MATTER WHAT PEOPLE TELL YOU,
WORDS AND IDEAS CAN CHANGE THE WORLD."
— ROBIN WILLIAMS

Later that year, the correctional officers made me consolidate cells with another Damu from Compton Piru named Rooster. Rooster was a lot bigger than I was, and he was already used to the prison system from a previous sentence. He had more experience than I did . From our very first interaction, I knew Rooster was full of pride and ego. He boasted about what he had and what he did in the streets, a typical way most hood dudes flaunt pictures of material objects they once had to try to appear relevant, especially to an impressionable youngster . I knew his personality traits well enough not to trust him, so I never spoke of anything of importance around him.

Something about Rooster rubbed me the wrong way from the moment we met. Although I was just 19, I had enough experience to recognize a certain personality type. It was a very common personality type on the streets, where we had to hustle for every dollar.

Whenever someone was particularly good at selling their product, there would always be people who were envious and wished to take that and monopolize it. This was Rooster in a nutshell. It showed in his pride and how he overtly showed off his belongings, the signs of his "success." I could tell that if I ever had something of my own, he would turn into a green-eyed monster fast.

Rooster was selfish, and that was made apparent when it was time to eat. I didn't have any money on my books when I entered the Los Angeles State Prison Reception Center, so I had to rely on eating the food that was served by the prison. Rooster would cook up meals from food he purchased from the commissary store and eat it in my face, leaving me feeling devalued and undermined. I remember one day, a letter from a pen pal came in the mail for me with a money order for $20.00. At the time, I owed restitution for injuries I caused to my victims, so the State of California took 45% of any money sent to me. I was left with $9.00 to spend at the commissary store, which isn't much at all.

I told Rooster how much money my pen pal sent me, and he burst into uncontrollable laughter, saying, "*Blood, what the fuck is twenty dollars? You won't even be able to buy a case of soup! You need to quit that bitch! HA HA HA HA HA.*"

He made me feel embarrassed. I was feeling angry that my family, at the least, didn't put money on my books to eat at the commissary store. I felt like a fool. The commissary store list was due to be turned in, so I analyzed my options. I knew if I thought about buying junk food, my money would be wasted. Instead, my hustler's mentality kicked in, and I searched up and down the store list, looking for items I could purchase that would flip and make a profit. Coffee popped into my brain. To me, it made perfect sense, especially considering that 85% of the prison population drank some form of caffeine. I made my move and bought an 8-ounce jar of Folgers coffee and a box of oatmeal.

As soon as that Folger jar of coffee got into my hands, I emptied the jar completely onto a sheet of paper, got a plastic bag from a porter, and cut it into even square pieces using a razor blade from my state-issued fishkit. A "fishkit" is the kit the prison officers give new inmates; it usually contains things like a very small toothbrush, comb, and toothpaste. I scooped a spoonful of Folgers coffee and secured it inside the plastic squares, then formed them into small plastic balls. I called them coffee balls, and I priced them at fifty cents. I wrote signs in pencil on a ripped piece of paper, placed tape on the back of the sign from an old county jail letter, and placed my coffee sign next to the water fountain advertising my new product.   Literally overnight, clientele started to emerge and new customers introduced themselves by name and gang. Not only was I receiving income, but I was receiving personal intel from allies and opposition to the Damu tribe. As I became more literate through reading, I understood the importance of gathering intelligence, especially on the opposition. I was amazed at how fast I made my money back plus profit! I couldn't believe how much money came pouring in. The beauty of it was that I was exchanging coffee for other commodity products, like soap, for example. Later, I would learn how to then transfer it into green dots that turn into real currency, good currency because it came through a righteous means. All of my physical needs were met at reception. My cellmate, Rooster, was just amazed by how it came pouring in. I remember him saying, "Them Jungle babies hustlers!" I had a proud moment and smiled at the compliment.

I filled my prison shelves with commissary food and cosmetics from the store. My cell number became so popular that correctional officers were noticing the traffic that was coming to the cell. It also became the subject of conversation between me and Rooster. He became jealous and paranoid, stating, "It looks like we are selling dope up here. I don't like to be on the hot spot."

I foresaw that being in the cell with Rooster was going to come with problems. The very next day, Rooster would catch a battery on staff case and be sent into a segregated housing unit, or, the hole, pending new criminal charges. I would soon be transported to Calipatria State Prison, aka, Death Valley.

Calipatria was known for its extreme heat and its extreme violence, thus the name 'Death Valley' became the nickname. I was obviously nervous about going to a place known for violence, but I was also beginning my journey inside this underworld, so it came with a bit of excitement. I entered the Calipatria State Prison intake unit where I had to be processed inside the system, which also came with the mandatory searches. I was placed in cell #225 right in front of the gun tower. My new cellmate was Scooby Ru from Inglewood Neighborhood Piru. At the time, he had been in prison for eighteen years, so he was experienced with the prison system. He took me under his wings and educated me about the rules of the yard and the politics of my new environment.

"Yard is mandatory; no exceptions for the YG`s," he stated with authority. "You must wear your shoes going to and from the showers."

I interrupted him and said, "Why is that? Why can't I wear my shower shoes when going to the shower or in the day-room?"

He responded strongly by raising his voice and deepening his tone, "Homie, if you want to survive prison and go home, then just comply with the rules."

I was speechless for a moment. Shortly after, the homie Set Trip from Bounty Hunters Watts Bloods came to the cell and introduced himself. He asked if I needed a care package since I had just arrived. I noticed that providing care packages was a known practice done with gang members and ethnic groups in prison. You have to be careful who you receive care packages from though, because sometimes they come with hidden obligations. That's something I later learned. Another homie by the name of Scrap from East Side Family Swans Bloods introduced himself to me as well.

Set Trip and Scrap were porters for the AM and PM shifts, so they were able to roam around the housing unit freely without being harassed by the correctional officers. Their position was to also transport lines of communication, food, cosmetics, and other goods for the Damu Blood tribe. I was the youngest in the entire yard at the time, so I did receive special attention from the homies, and it felt good to be embraced by real, reputable ones.

I remember one day I was in the cell stressing over not receiving a package and a TV from my family, and Scrap came to the cell and noticed my mood was down. Getting a TV in prison meant that we had to show good behavior beforehand. We weren't allowed to watch R rated movies and programs that show excessive violence and blood. Usually, when an inmate got a TV sent to them by friends or family, it got checked and screened before the inmate received it.

"Young Blood, why are you stressing? You are too blessed to be stressed," Scrap said, with a grin on his face. "I'm waiting on my package to get here with my TV, " I responded back in a low tone. "The best TV you can have is right outside your cell door," he continued. "This TV is not watered down or filtered. Observation in prison is one of your best friends, young Black Stone. Next to observation is always listening to the tier."

Scrap was a very wise and articulate man. I admired these traits about him. The lesson of observation became essential for me in prison. I would watch and observe people for hours out of a day. I became so good at it that I knew the movements of people without even looking at them. As soon as their cell came open, I began to calculate and predict where they would go. It became like a little game I would play with my cellmate, Scooby. He would verify if I was right or wrong. Oftentimes, I was right because I learned that human beings are creatures of habit.

Dynamite from Oak Park Bloods came to the cell and introduced himself to me and brought me a care package equipped with a book. "What's brackin' young Black Stone, you read?" He asked in a very energetic tone. *"Yeah, I read, big homie. What you got for me?"* I asked with the same tone of voice. "The Browder File by Anthony Browder, this what imma start you off with. Check it out and I'll be at you in a week."

He slid the book underneath the cell and disappeared. I glanced at the book and immediately noticed the African symbols and a Pharaoh on the cover. I didn't know what to think about the book because history was not my favorite subject at all. During my younger days, there wasn't much of a reason for me to even want to study history because it reminded me of the unfortunate conditions of slavery

Black people endured, and every time I was reminded, I would get angry.

"Be prepared to have a discussion and write an essay about that book," Scooby said from his cell bunk. "A discussion and an essay? What the fuck?" I fired back. "Why do I have to have a discussion and write an essay?" I asked. "Because it proves you've read the book and are willing to learn," answered Scooby.

The homies were testing me in several different areas. Unbeknownst to me, I was starting my training sessions as a soldier in the yard. It included but was not limited to physical, mental, emotional, and cultural training practices. I would learn Swahili in order to participate in group workouts with the homies. I would learn weaponry by manufacturing prison knives. I would learn ambush formations in preparation for large-scale riots. I would learn how to read and write at an academic level to hold down political discussions. I would watch and pay attention to how my homies de-escalated tense situations with other races to learn diplomacy. My mind was young, fresh, and fertile, so these lessons I was learning were turning me into a grown man at a young age; I had just turned 21. At that time, I was more focused on learning the rules of my environment.

Hustling coffee wasn't my focus at the time, but I noticed how coffee was a big part of prison life. Homies would start their day off with a fresh cup of Folgers at 4:00 am. Coffee would be used to begin workouts, read books, play chess, and engage in conversations. I understood very clearly that coffee could be used as a medium to interact with all sorts of people. Instead of hustling coffee at the time, I used coffee to leverage relationships with Crips, Bloods, Mexicans, and Whites. I knew coffee was Black Gold in prison. Inmates went to the extent of putting coffee in prison-made gin called "white lighting," mixing the two together, creating a concoction called "Black Russian." This proved to be a recipe for disaster, as 90% of those who dared to take a shot ended up causing an incident involving violence.

The mix of confined people and a shot of caffeine and alcohol was a bad one. But it wasn't just a spark for trouble, or a way to stay alert. Coffee was also a means of spiritual retreat. Religious brothers used coffee to begin the process of scribing down sermons inspired to uplift the souls of the oppressed and downtrodden. I started to study coffee more in depth and discovered that coffee is a fruit that grows on cherry trees. I wondered why it was called a bean if it came from a fruit. The natives thought it looked like a bean, so they called it one.

The coffee plant is in an entirely different family of plants than legumes. What we know as "coffee beans" are actually seeds of the coffee berry. In fact, coffee originated in Ethiopia. According to legend, the story goes that Kaldi discovered coffee after he noticed that after eating the berries from a certain tree, his goats became so energetic that they did not want to sleep at night. In the legend, Kaldi was an Ethiopian goat herder around 850 A.D.

Kaldi reported his findings to the abbot of the local monastery, who made a drink with the berries and found that it kept him alert through the long hours of evening prayer. The abbot shared his discovery with the other monks at the monastery, and knowledge of the energizing berries began to spread. It then became a drink of choice amongst monks, mystics, sufis, and other people of knowledge used to engaging in spiritual and intellectual discourse. Kaldi would bring coffee to the monks for prayer, so coffee was thus revealed to mankind to connect to the spiritual realm and keep them awake. It would later be associated with being the fuel of the creator. From

Ethiopia to Yemen and throughout the world, coffee has become famous. And over a millennium later, the influence of coffee stayed strong, businesses have been started and grounded on coffee.

Coffee has become associated with Islamic narratives. One narrative mentions the Angel Gabriel introducing coffee to the Prophet Muhammad (May peace be upon him) for the sake of weaning humanity away from wine and other intoxicants. It was important for me to receive that knowledge because it had now made me feel connected to divinity. I felt good selling people a product that was good for them, unlike the crack or crystal meth that I used to sell.

ANTHONY MCDUFFIE JR.

CHAPTER 7

SPIRITUAL AWAKENING

"PEACE CANNOT BE ACHIEVED THROUGH VIOLENCE;
IT CAN ONLY BE ATTAINED THROUGH UNDERSTANDING."
- RALPH WALDO EMERSON

As time went on, I was gaining knowledge, but I wasn't gaining spiritual healing conducive to healing my soul and heart from years of compounded trauma. I was starting to surround myself with self-proclaimed scholars and intellectuals, while straddling the fence with some of the most violent Bloods in the California Penal Code system. It was a healthy tug of war between two competing forces: good and evil. I learned balance, straddling the fence of good and evil. Most of the intellectuals I hung around with just so happened to be Muslim. Initially, I thought Islam was a religion for Arabs, and Allah was the name of the Arab God. I grew up in a Christian household, so images of white Jesus were hung around the house, but accepting a white man to be my God just didn't sit well with my spirit.

I didn't claim any religion at the time, although I prayed to a God. Whatever you entertain most can become your God. I was entertaining street politics and involving myself in gang affairs. I became very manipulative over time and learned how to manipulate women to do my bidding. I finessed a young female pen pal to bring me drugs through the visiting room. I was inexperienced in drug smuggling, so my first attempt at it failed miserably. It landed me in the hole, pending investigation in solitary confinement. I was looking at an additional charge. I remember feeling guilty about my actions. I realized I had caused a negative ripple effect in another person's life by tarnishing her civil reputation. She was listed as a felon and spent jail time away from her family. I was on a potty watch. A potty watch process is used to recover drugs, weapons, cellphones, and other contraband that inmates are believed to have swallowed or concealed in body cavities.

Suspected smugglers are put in isolation cells with their hands chained and sometimes covered in "hand isolation devices" similar to oven mitts. Their clothing is taped shut to keep them from reaching the body cavities. They remain there for at least 72 hours or until they have at least three bowel movements. Due to this situation, I was shackled from waist to feet in a cell with a bright light on for 24 hours. It felt like torture because I wasn't able to sleep. Sleep deprivation caused my body to become weak.

After six months of investigation, the DA decided to reject the case due to an insignificant amount of drugs. I was discharged from the hole and placed back into the general population. A-yard became my temporary housing unit.   As soon as I arrived in the yard, an older brother walking around the track yelled out at me to get my attention, "Say young brother, I noticed you from a distance. You're a hidden gem! What city are you from?" "I'm from LA," I responded right back.

"My name is Ahmed, my young brother, from San Diego. It's a pleasure to meet you." I was thrown back by the hospitality. Brother

Ahmed complimented me within the first 60 seconds of knowing me. He definitely made a great first impression, and in the weeks to follow, we would begin to have discussions about all sorts of topics, from religion to politics. He began to teach me how to be a hunter and hunt for knowledge. I would start to devour scholarly books from prominent authors such as Van Sertima in his book entitled "They Came Before Columbus" and Na'im Akbar in his book entitled "Visions for Black Men." I was receiving visions in my third eye as I became enlightened and awakened. It was an actual physical, mental, and spiritual phenomenon. The way I was receiving this newfound knowledge felt mystical. That was great and all, but I was also feeling low as I was constantly short of money, so I was hustling to get food and toiletries for myself because money being sent from my family slowed up.

Hustling coffee was back in full effect. I began hustling Muslim incense as well. Prayer oil from religious packages was a hot commodity. Having built relationships with the Muslim community put me in touch with quality prayer oil that was sold at $100 for 4 oz. Muslim prayer oil was used to cover up scents like weed, crystal meth, poor hygiene odor, and any other foul smells.

I switched into a hustle mentality like Kobe Bryant switching into the Mamba Mentality. At that point in time, I was hyper-focused on making money. I figured out how to make more money by selling coffee. I would learn the new monetary system of Green Dots. By activating an account, I was given a debit Visa card that I had sent to my brother's house and ordered special purchase packages in my name. I would order 16 oz jars of Folgers coffee at $10 a jar. I then would wait strategically for a lockdown to happen, because they always did, and then sell a jar for $50, quadrupling my profit. I would make enough money to support myself and cellmates the I had at the time. I would even be able to pay off the remainder of my restitution.

During yard, I remember a brother coming around with a sign-up list, signing people up for an Arabic class. I was interested from the very beginning. In Calipatria, there was literally nothing for the youth to do besides workout all day and escape our unfortunate reality through using some form of drug, so I saw learning another language as a benefit. I noticed the people that were mostly signing up for Arabic class were Muslim, besides me and an older homie named Dicky Berg from Bounty Hunters Watts Bloods. I was nervous at first because of the perception my peers had of me . They saw me as the active gang member on the frontlines of the Damu tribe, which I was, but I also had an intellectual side that I hid. There wasn't much respect given to intellectuals by the gang members, so I had to cultivate my intellect in the shadows of my own cell.

Attending the first class session of Arabic, I noticed I was the only youth in attendance. Before class actually started, the brothers around me centered themselves on a Muslim prayer rug, and the call to prayer was made . I was 25 when I finally began to embrace religion. Not being a Muslim at the time, I was reluctant to pray with them, but then I was directed by Dickey Berg to join the formation. Not knowing what to do, I motioned to Dickey Berg that I didn't know how to pray, and he told me to just copy what I saw the Muslims do, so I did.

It felt awkward to pray to a God I knew nothing about. Strangely enough, I felt something activating within me as I made the prayer. I was taught according to a hierarchical structure, so the military-type formation for prayer, with one man leading, appealed to me. After prayer was done, we all sat down, and I watched the brothers all lift their palms in the air at the same time and begin uttering words in Arabic that onceI heard my Uncle Stevie once say in the holding tanks in the Los Angeles County Jail to a Middle Eastern man. I found out that what the brothers were saying was the 'Al-Fatiha,' which means "The Opening." The Al-Fatiha is also the first chapter of the Holy Quran, and Muslims collectively utter the Al-Fatiha for protection from evil and guidance from God to embark upon the spiritual journey. The Al-Fatiha is so important to Muslims that they recite it seventeen times a day during each of the five prayers they are obligated to perform.

Once we were done reciting the Al-Fatiha, we began our first lesson by using Arabic words from the Holy Quran. This threw me back for a second, because I had no idea that this Arabic class was religion-based, but as we started to dive into the grammatical structure and learn about the different characters that represented each word, I was immediately pulled in. I became fascinated by how vast the Arabic language was. Not only did it capture my complete attention, but I found it to be interactive and poetic in flow.

As I learned more about the language, I also learned more about the religion, so much so that I began to recite the prayer to myself. I also started to learn about the different names of God, like Al-Rahman, which in Arabic means "The Merciful." I thought it was fascinating to know about different names of God and the attributes that govern each name because, growing up in a Christian household, the only name I heard associated with God was Jesus. I was being introduced to new spiritual knowledge that sat right with my spirit. I felt my heart, mind, and soul expanding with this new information.

The more I studied, the more my soul began to purify itself. I was having a spiritual awakening and I felt it.

I was tapping into divinity like I was trained to do through years upon years of in-depth study. I understood the ancient adage, "Know thyself." I was getting to know myself, and to know myself meant knowing my creator. Islam just so happened to be my pathway.

CHAPTER 8

SELF REHABILITATION

"IT IS DURING OUR DARKEST MOMENTS THAT
WE MUST FOCUS TO SEE THE LIGHT."
— ARISTOTLE

Rehabilitation begins inwardly. Once I was taken out of the matrix, out of the reality of South Central LA and placed in a prison cell away from society and the distractions of society, I began to see how lost I was. A lot of what I was taught was self-hate, leading to and contributing to the mass genocide of Black people. Once I became conscious of that reality, I had to change that mentality, and it started with me. I had to redefine myself, not as a Black soldier, active gang leader, or smart criminal, but as a servant to the Creator of a Higher Order. I see my human experience as a borrowed experience shared with others, only to test who is best amongst us to do good deeds. Indeed, this is true in the way of good currency; when you do good, you earn good.

I had been transferred to Lancaster State Prison from Calipatria when I was 29. There I was reintroduced to my spiritual mentor and guide, Tobias, aka Ibn Wali Shakir. By decree, we were placed in the cell together. We redefined the cell and turned it into a cave for healing and rehabilitation, sort of like Plato did. This was when I started accepting the concept of self-help, and when I started it, I dove right in.

According to Plato, one prisoner could become free if he sees the fire and realizes that the shadows are fake. This prisoner escapes from the cave and discovers that there is a whole new world outside that he was previously unaware of. The prisoner believes that the outside world is so much more real than the world of shadows in the cave. He tries to return to free the other prisoners. Upon his return, he is temporarily blinded because his eyes are not accustomed to actual sunlight and are trying to readjust.

The chained prisoners see this blindness and believe that they would be harmed if they tried to leave the cave. The prisoners grow wary about stepping into the light and stick to the familiar darkness, which is their comfort zone. God sent Tobias to train me on how to leave the cave and discover new worlds. Tobias gave me Quranic formulas I would use to help uplift my spirit and heal my soul from years of compounded trauma. Tobias would become instrumental in the process of building my confidence while destroying my ego.

We spent months philosophizing and dissecting sociology books through the utilizition of a spiritual filter. He gave me the proper structure that I needed. I also regarded him as my father figure and mentor. My mentor's name is actually a legendary name, and according to legend, his name was in the first of the stolen books of the Bible. The book itself is one of the most delightful books of Hebrew Scripture. The book is a religious novel characterized as a Hebrew romance and is a captivating narrative. The book begins with the father who shares a name with my mentor, an Israelite of the Northern Kingdom deported to Nineveh who suffers from blindness. Sara in

Medes suffers torment. Because of their good life and prayers, God sends the Archangel Raphael to help them. The virtuous son (who also shares a name with my mentor) joins the disguised Raphael on a journey to Medes on his father's behalf, and brings happiness both to his father and Sara.

Tobias became the inner city beacon of hope and the revolutionary leader of the disenfranchised, marginalized, and poor. He brought light and power of influence. I felt safe and secure around him. He trained me in spiritual sacred knowledge and the training consisted of "The Khafi Boy Experience," where we would read Surah 18 from the Holy Quran, which required profound reflection and contemplation. The verse of reflection from the Holy Quran begins with Allah asking the reader:

"Do you consider, think, reckon that the people of the cave and the inscriptions were a miracle among our signs? Allah continued. When the youths fled for refuge as a quest into the cave, they said, "Our Lord! Bestow on us mercy from yourself, and help facilitate our affairs the right way." (Quran 18:9-10)

I see this verse as important and relevant to today's current social epidemic plight, especially with the inner-city youth. The social conditions of youth in present times are the same as those referred to in the Holy Scripture. A process of socialization was absolutely necessary and needed for me to correct prior patterns of social learning that were detrimental. The transition whereby I underwent intense, major changes in belief systems and behavioral patterns became a spiritual process of reforming, rehabilitating, and reconstructing my social being, beginning with my soul first. I started to become God-Conscious. I prayed more, fasted more, and studied more. Tobias advised us to take advantage of the self-help classes and the educational system as well. I enrolled in college, taking sociology courses and analyzing social dynamics through an Islamic filter. I also began taking self-help courses to better understand myself.

I met Lee Gibson during this transition. Lee, along with Dartell Williams, created a self-help class called "Helping Youth Offenders Understand Their Harm." In this class, Lee facilitated information for me that was transformative. I learned about new concepts such as triggers, causative factors, and ripple effects. I learned about the impact I caused on my community and the communities of others through my acts of violence. In learning, about the importance of taking responsibility for making a poor choice or bad decision in life, I learned about remorse and why remorse is necessary to heal my wounded inner child. I learnt about empathy, compassion, and forgiveness. I learnt that to make amends for my past crimes, I had to start with a changed lifestyle. My change had to come from within and then spread outwards to the people around me.

It was in this class that I had enough courage to speak openly about traumatic experiences such as sexual abuse that I had suppressed within myself. It was the first time I saw men speak openly about their emotions without judgment. It made me feel accepted. It felt good to be a part of a positive peer group. I learned about the process of victimization and that being a victimizer is a learned behavior that stems from being victimized by someone else. Lee Gibson and all of the brothers that helped support "Helping Youth Offenders Understand Their Harm" created a space for growth, safety, and healing.

The class was a parole board hearing prep class. This class was pivotal because it prepared me in ways I didn't realize at the time. We learned that thousands of men and women were being denied parole due to a lack of insight into their crimes, a lack of remorse, and a lack of parole plans. The Board of Parole Hearings had a strict process where inmates underwent an intense hearing involving two commissioners, a district attorney, a public or private defense attorney, and the family of the victims in attendance. The commissioners, along with the district attorney, drill inmates in a stern way with a sequence of questions about their upbringing, adolescent years, involvement with drugs or gangs, the crime that caused their conviction, behavior while locked up, self-help classes, and parole plans. Inmates not only had to articulate themselves to the board's standards, but they also had to maintain a passive, slave-like demeanor throughout the entire hearing. Failure to meet any of the standards provided by the CDCR's Board of Parole Hearings resulted in a 3, 5, 7 or 10-year denial of parole.

The process was crude and intimidating for most inmates. In fact, most inmates would postpone their hearings for years out of fear of being denied. I often felt that the Board of Parole was being unrealistic with its expectations. Requiring inmates to remain disciplinary-free for at least three years is a miracle considering the nature of prison, and the pressure of dealing with prison politics, racism, thousands of moody attitudes, and correctional officers; it's a miracle if you are found to be suitable for parole. I will be forever grateful to have gone through such a rehabilitative process. I absorbed so much self-help information that I started to become a better version of myself. I was then able to facilitate what I had learned with others. I became a facilitator for the Alternative to Violence Project, GOGI, Islamic Health & Fitness, and several other self-help classes. I had enough training and experience to train, assist, support, and inspire my peers. I was going through a metamorphosis of self-rehabilitation.

I entered into the Paws for Life dog program by way of Dennis Smith, who just so happened to be my cellmate and Tobias's co-defendant. Working with rescued dogs on the brink of euthanization who were dealing with behavioral issues like impulsivity, reminded me of myself. In fact, I saw the dog no differently than how I saw myself, so I saw the dog in me. Just as I felt deserving of attention, love, and affection, so did the dogs I was responsible for taking care of. I saw how training a dog is similar to training a human being. Positive reward systems produce the best results. I learned patience, kindness, and openness for myself, but that also had to translate to other living beings. I had to be considerate to understand that other living beings are sharing an earthly experience with me, and they are deserving of respect. I felt connected to my humanity again.

CHAPTER 9

"FOR ME, BECOMING ISN'T ABOUT ARRIVING SOMEWHERE OR
ACHIEVING A CERTAIN AIM. I SEE IT INSTEAD AS FORWARD MOTION,
A MEANS OF EVOLVING, A WAY TO REACH CONTINUOUSLY TOWARD
A BETTER SELF. THE JOURNEY DOESN'T END."
— MICHELLE OBAMA

When I was 33, I was released from prison. I had spent 15 years
in total in prison, and although I was a bit nervous, I was not alone. I
was picked up by Tobias, my old prison cellmate, and my two brothers, Terell and Brian. I was super excited to see my brothers and my
spiritual leader at the exit point of the State Prison. I went immediately into prostration, thanking the good God Almighty for my freedom. I felt elated. The air of freedom felt different and refreshing in a
way. I jumped in the car and was driven to see my sweet mother after
fifteen years. As soon as I saw her, I ran to her and I melted inside her
arms. I waited a long time to see, hear, and touch my mother. I spent
time catching up with her and my Auntie Reather.

During my time in prison and my metamorphosis, my mindset had changed, and so did my relationship with my mother. During my self-help sessions, I learned a lot about depression, addiction, and abuse. This helped me realize that I had to cut her some slack, and she was dealing with a lot while trying to keep our home together. Empathizing with her made me understand her, and this meant that I was finally able to let go of my resentment. I made amends with her, and as I sank into her arms in a warm, comforting hug, I was glad that I had.

Shortly after, Tobias wanted to take me to the Hot & Cool Cafe branch in Leimert Park to reunite with my other little brothers, whom I hadn't seen or talked to in a very long time. Bion, Jabari, Brian, and Terell were all present to welcome me home. I felt elated and high on life. We created such a powerful and loving presence through our embracing of one another that it attracted Big Boy, the entertainer from the Power 106 radio station. This guy is legendary in the Southland. I grew up listening to his pranks as a teenager. I was also embraced by locals who came out of the stores to clap at us hugging.

One brother shouted, "*We need to see more young brothers out here showing love to each other like this!*" We definitely created a positive vibe. I was then introduced to Trey Jo, a DC native, Black entrepreneur, CEO of Crenshaw Coffee Co. and Hot & Cool Cafe. He would later become my mentor and teach me the nature of coffee. It felt divine, like some alignment was forming.

Tobias reminded me about attending Jummah services and everything related to my faith. He took my religious growth very seriously. 'Jummah' means "to gather" or "summon" in Arabic. A Jummah prayer is when Muslims congregate for congregational devotion during Friday midday prayer. It is known as "Jummah." An imam delivers a sermon (khutbah) after the prayer.

It is the day on which believing, practicing Muslims gather to worship The One God. I was so honored and grateful to attend my first Jummah service as a free man. I gave thanks and praise to The One God and felt blessed. God had delivered me from the depths of hell on Earth. Our services were fulfilling and always gave me inner peace.

The question was asked, "Are you acclimated to this new way of living?" I had to define "acclimated." Acclimated means to become accustomed to a new climate or new conditions. Well, let's see, I was paroled on the eve of the murder of legendary Los Angeles rapper, Nipsey Hussle, in the summer of 2019, to a transitional housing facility in downtown Los Angeles on 8th and San Pedro, a street also known as Skid Row. It was a cesspool of Los Angeles' underworld for the downtrodden. This street was known to house parolees and people with multiple addictions and mental illnesses.

I was placed in a building called the Weingart Center. My first encounter with the building consisted of a fight that broke out between two elderly ladies over staring. Although I had seen many fights, it still felt jarring to see one started over something so small. And this was outside prison. I didn't think people would be so volatile outside prison walls. I knew then that I was placed in an unsafe environment. Ten minutes after that encounter, an ambulance came speeding down the street for an incident that happened 200 yards away. I remember placing my back against the wall of the building in defense. Every day after that, I literally went to sleep and woke up to cop sirens. I was placed in a room that had bed bugs in it. I was attacked by bed bugs and suffered from itchy bite marks all over my body. Bed bugs were in all my clothes as well. My clothes were now compromised. I thought about the treatment I received. As a parolee, I received a $10 gift card for Target from my parole agent to buy me clothes for a job interview.

After I complained several times to my parole agent about not having enough money to even buy a shirt, he finally came clean with me and told me that the department didn't have any more funds to give to parolees. I felt naked, dependent, and powerless. I had no documentation of proof of my identity besides my prison I.D. I had no transportation and no sense of direction. The California Department of Corrections and Rehabilitation failed me miserably. They clearly had no plans for rehabilitation for me when they sent me to Skid Row to be confronted with all of my fears, PTSD, and anxiety. Reentry into society should begin with a healing phase because we must truly heal ourselves from years of incarceration in order to present ourselves in the best way. Years of incarceration made me institutionalized, so I think that it would be imperative to deprogram anyone coming from prison. Apparently, the California Department of Corrections didn't feel that way about me.

Every day I felt like I was walking through the night of the living dead. There was a certain resident evil that took place every night, and no one was safe. I was aware of all the wars going on in the streets. The city was under a purge. I looked at everything as a potential threat or danger. I had to see a psychologist because my post-traumatic stress disorder and anxiety overwhelmed my mind.

After I came to the realization that the 'Department of Mental Health' in Los Angeles just wanted to medicate me into coping with my unfortunate circumstances, I stopped going to mental health sessions and decided to figure things out on my own.

I was sent to The Cavanagh House transitional for about seven months. During the Cavanagh House experience, I got a phone call from my auntie in the wee hours of the morning, telling me that my little brother was just shot and killed. I received this on the day of my birthday. I was devastated by the news. Mentally and emotionally, I was broken down and shaken. The Cavanagh House did provide better care than the Weingarzt, but it also came with its own restrictive policies that weren't, in my opinion, conducive to my rehabilitation, considering what I was dealing with at the time. However, I was grateful to God that I was away from the Weingarzt.

I acquired all of my documentation proving my citizenship and began working at a warehouse. I would save up every paycheck, understanding that I needed to start becoming independent and join the working industrial society. Financial literacy was the key to my financial freedom, so I started to build my credit profile. I had enough credit to earn a brand new Dodge Challenger, fresh from the car dealership. I had saved enough money from coffee balls to open up several bank accounts. I was wise enough to know not to burn all my money on bullshit. I used the money to finance my first apartment as a free man. I enrolled in college, and began my first summer semester at Cal State Los Angeles. I felt good about my small accomplishments and achievements. Things were going well until a potentially world ending pandemic struck.

In March 2020, the COVID-19 pandemic shut down the entire world, and at the time, I was working at a women's shelter. There was no protocol or safety health regulations in place at the time, so the shelter would have COVID-19 outbreaks often. I realized the company wasn't working in the interest of the employees to protect us from the virus, and, as a result, we were putting our lives on the line, so I quit.

Depending on my personal savings to support me for the time being, I was in need of work. God must have heard my prayers, because a few months later, I would be included in a meeting at Hot & Cool Cafe with Tobias and Trey Jo that would give me the skill set and mindset to become a boss. The first lesson I had to learn was self-development. I had to conquer my fear of failing when trying to succeed. I had to conquer my fear of doubting the process.

Three weeks later, I started to work at the coffee shop on Slauson, in the heart of the Rollin 60's Crips territory. Business was good, so I was busy getting everything ready, especially during rush hour. I had to conquer the fear of the boundaries of preconceived rivals, knowing I was protected by Allah, which was the ultimate lesson. At the coffee shop, I learned how to sort coffee beans, prepare coffee beans for roasting with traditional Ethiopian prayers upon the beans, grind coffee, package coffee, brew coffee, mass roast coffee, and profile coffee. I worked at the Hot & Cool Cafe to learn the etiquette of how to run a cafe. I was now a conqueror of fear and a master of the art of coffee.

Currently, I am part of a corporation called 'Good Currency Studios,' and our global movement is to do good and earn good for humanity. I'm a film/podcast producer there, and my work feels very fulfilling. My mission is to bring back the good in the world, starting with a cup of coffee to connect humanity to the source of good, which is Allah, The One God. I'm in the moment of manifesting all the good in my life while speaking about my life. I went down the wrong path earlier in life, just like most troubled youth in the inner-city of South Central Los Angeles. I took the lemons that life gave me and made lemonade. I took the initiative to address my traumas, pain, and inner suffering to become a beacon of hope for those I could direct towards a positive way of life. I was striving to fail in a gang culture that rewards failure, but I ended up becoming a success story. I am so grateful that God made me to be a light in the valley of darkness and death.

CHAPTER 10

REFLECTIONS

"YOU DEFINE YOUR OWN LIFE. DON'T LET OTHER PEOPLE WRITE YOUR SCRIPT."
— OPRAH WINFREY

During my long years of incarceration, I was able to tap out of the matrix of gangs and crime, tap into my inner self, and refine my character. Many lessons were learned, but one that stuck with me the most was that I was worth the effort to change. I found value in myself to have the confidence to step into a new life of positivity. I was dealing with adverse childhood experiences that led me to a life of gangs and crime. I was reckless, impulsive, violent, angry, and a menace to society. I did not have a sense of direction or purpose for my life. From juvenile halls, Los Angeles County Jail, to State Prison, I maintained a blind obedience to a gang that would have turned on me at the snap of a finger if I did anything to violate the gang code.

During those pivotal years of incarceration, I found myself and started investing in myself. I built up the confidence to value my self-worth and make decisions that would enrich my life. Undergoing the process of rehabilitation, and taking several self-help classes, I felt transformed in my thoughts, behaviors, and actions. I felt good about the positivity I was allowing to come into my life. I felt like I was reconnecting myself to humanity. I realized through those long years of incarceration that my identity was beyond the personality that I had created within the gang culture; it was tied to an enriched history in Africa. I have a spirit and a soul connected to Mother Earth that is having an earthly experience. I've learned virtues such as patience, tolerance, and respect for all beings living amongst me. I've learned that life comes with struggles, hardships, and obstacles. How I choose to respond determines my outcome. Positive thoughts and positive words lead to positive actions.

I've moved past that bad part of my life and I've become more conscious about making decisions that can affect my life or the lives of others. For that reason, I focused on my studies. I received all A's in my courses at Cal State Los Angeles. I've chosen to work with the homeless. I work with women's homeless shelters, hoping that I can give someone the help I wish I had gotten when I was a runaway. Just as I was mentored and put on a better path, I hope to do the same for others. I'm part of an organization that mentors youths in the inner city with gang prevention and intervention as our goals. The goal is to help these youths before they get into the prison system. With this in mind, I do empowerment speeches in youth centers all over Southern California.

I also reflect intimately on the Lil Dogg or underdogs in marginalized communities such as the Baldwin Hills Village that may or may not have gang ties. I'm here to tell you that you can change your environment by changing your mind-state. You create your own reality! In the net of imagination, you can manifest whatever you want in life. You have to believe in yourself when no one else will. You have to believe in your own magic! If you believe you're trapped, then you're trapped, but if you believe you're free, then you're free!

Be free from the criticism of your peers. Be free from the violence done on Black or Brown people. Be free from the hate and judgment of society. Just be you and you will be free.

I'll leave you with words said by Prophet Mohammad (May peace be upon him) to his companions."If the world were ending before your eyes but you held a sapling in your hands, plant it! Don't be concerned with its fate. Your task is to plant."

ANTHONY MCDUFFIE JR.

PHOTO GALLERY

THREE YEARS OLD INNOCENT AND EXPERIENCING JOY
WITH BOTH MY PARENTS

ME AND MY LITTLE BROTHER TERELL BEING CARE GIVERS
FOR MY FATHER WHO LOST HIS VISION.

ANTHONY MCDUFFIE JR.

FIRST YEAR IN PRISON STRESSED OUT

RECEIVING SMALL SUCCESS SELLING COFFEE BALLS AT 50 CENT A PIECE

ANTHONY MCDUFFIE JR.

BEING UNITED AFTER 15 YEARS WITH MY MOTHER AND AUNTIE REATHER

BEING UNITED WITH MY BROTHERS AT THE
HOT & COOL CAFE FRESH OUT OF PRISON

DISCHARGING PAROLE AND FINALLY FEELING FREE!

WORKING AT THE COFFEE SHOP

SPEAKING TO YOUTH AT A YOUTH CENTER

PRODUCING PODCAST FOR GOOD CURRENCY

ANTHONY MCDUFFIE JR.

NEED HELP ON RE ENTRY?

WANT TO HELP SOMEONE RE ENTERING?

Good Currency Studios is a B Corporation that highlights documentaries, stories, podcast, and film shows of marginalized communities giving them a platform to share their experiences with the world. 10% of all proceeds go to charities

For more information on how to get involved with Good Currency Studios or it's re-entry endeavors, please contact Livin@GoodCurrency.org

ANTHONY MCDUFFIE JR.

Made in the USA
Middletown, DE
26 May 2022

66221503R00057